WORD FAMILY TALES™

Teaching Guide

Word Family Tales -ack
A Snack for Mack
by Cass Hollander
Illustrated by Rick Brown

Word Family Tales -ip
Take a Trip to Planet Blip
by Kama Einhorn
Illustrated by Matt Phillips

Word Family Tales -op
Bop, Bop at the Bunny Hop
by Robin C. Fitzsimmons
Illustrated by Ellen Joy Sasaki

Lessons, Word Family Activities & Reproducible Mini-Book Versions of All 25 Storybooks

SCHOLASTIC
PROFESSIONAL BOOKS

New York • Toronto • London • Auckland • Sydney • New Delhi • Mexico City • Hong Kong • Buenos Aires

For Theo and Dash

Activities written by Wiley Blevins and Joan Novelli
Cover design by Andrew Drew and interior design by Norma Ortiz

ISBN: 0-439-26248-8

Table of Contents

Teaching with Word Family Tales

The Mini-Books

Certificate of Completion

A Note to Teachers

What do cat, hat, sat, and bat have in common? They all belong to the same family—word family, that is. Word families, also known as phonograms, can offer you an efficient way to boost children's early reading skills. The beauty of word families lies in the fact that nearly 500 simple, primary-grade words can be derived from a very small set of word families. Another value of word families is that they are reliable and generalizable—most are pronounced and spelled the same in every word in which they appear. Knowing these word families will allow your child to get the most out of phonics instruction. Teaching children how to recognize these word families will improve their ability to sound out and spell words.

Word families have frequently been used in spelling instruction because word patterns are the most effective vehicle for teaching spelling. Word families have also been used to provide a boost to early reading instruction. Many children enter first grade with a fair grasp of consonants and the sounds they represent. By learning a word family such as –at, they can generate a number of primary-level words such as bat, cat, fat, hat, mat, pat, rat, and sat. Children can then use these words in early independent writing. And, children will encounter these words while reading many primary-level stories.

Teaching children that words contain recognizable chunks and teaching them to search for these word parts or patterns is an important step to developing reading fluency. As children encounter more and more multisyllabic words, he or she will gain an understanding that words may contain recognizable parts (word families, suffixes, prefixes, smaller words). This insight is critical for decoding the words quickly and efficiently.

Activities such as reading and identifying word families in poetry and stories, using familiar word parts to sound out an unknown word, creating word family word walls or charts, and building words using word families can enhance your child's understanding of how words work and improve children's overall literacy skills. Besides, they're also a lot of fun!

Enjoy!

Wiley Blevins
Ed.M. Harvard University

Welcome to Word Family Tales!

Learning to read is an exciting and important accomplishment for any child. It's a gift we give children that will forever change their lives. Much can be done to speed up a child's reading progress. Word Family Tales offer an effective way to capitalize on child's interest in rhyme and word play. They can also enhance a child's developing understanding of how words "work." Each humorous read-aloud story in the *Word Family Tales* collection introduces children to a new word family, such as the –at family (found in cat, bat, hat, sat, and mat). The program contains one book for each of the 25 most frequently used word families. Reading and spelling words with these word families will boost children's literacy skills and provide a fun, valuable reading experience.

Other features of the *Word Family Tales* program are:

◆ an easy-to-learn word family cheer designed to help children remember the word family spelling pattern as well as to celebrate learning

◆ reading tips that provide a quick and fun way to use the story to strengthen children's skills and assess his or her progress

◆ word family riddles at the end of the story that challenge children to generate words using context clues and their knowledge of the word family's spelling pattern

◆ mini-book versions of all 25 stories to give children further exposure and practice with each word family.

Teaching Tips

Keep these tips in mind as you introduce and share the *Word Family Tales* books.

✶1 Choosing the Sequence

There is no one correct order for using the *Word Family Tales* books. However, there is a sequence that will be easier for children to grasp the concept of word families and build on previous learning. Start with the short vowel word families, such as –at and –ap, then progress to long vowel word families, such as –ice and –eep. This is a sequence commonly used in elementary reading programs. Below is the suggested sequence.

-at	-in	-ack	-ing	-ice
-ap	-ip	-ock	-ink	-ide
-an	-ug	-uck	-ank	-eep
-ot	-ell	-ump	-ake	-ail
-op	-est	-ill	-ine	-ay

✱ 2 Before Reading

Introduce the story and word family featured in each *Word Family Tales* book using one or all of the following activities.

◆ Show the cover of the book. Read aloud the title and author and illustrator's name. Have children look at a few pages of the book. Ask: What do you think this book will be about? What might we learn from reading this book? What pictures or characters look interesting? Why?

◆ Introduce the word family. Point to the word family's spelling pattern on the cover. Spell aloud and pronounce the word family. For example, "The letters a-t make the /at/ sound. We will find this word family in words such as cat and hat. Can you think of any other words with the /at/ sound?" Encourage children to spell the words generated.

◆ Skim the book with children and look for words containing the word family. Have children point to them as you read them together.

✱ 3 During Reading

The first time through, just read the selected *Word Family Tales* book aloud. This will allow children time to enjoy the story and get a feel for the language. Get more out of the story with these tips:

◆ Reread the story, this time asking children to look and listen for the featured word family. Let children signal when they hear the word family at the end of the word—for example, by holding up a card on which the word family is written.

◆ On another reading of the story, ask children to closely examine the illustration on each page. Do they see anything pictured whose name contains the word family? Can they find the name for this object in the text?

◆ After several readings, encourage children to chime in on predictable words, especially words containing the word family. You may need to pause before the word as you point to it to help your child. Children will delight in seeing how many words they know.

✱ 4 After Reading

Extend the learning with activities that build on the *Word Family Tales* story.

◆ Play a quick game to reinforce the word family. For example, state a word with the word family's spelling pattern, such as cat for the –at word family. Then have children generate as many words as possible that rhyme with cat. Write the words on paper and have children circle the –at spelling pattern.

◆ Have fun with the cheer that accompanies each *Word Family Tales* book. After practicing the original cheer, let children make up a new cheer. Write the cheer on paper, leaving blanks for each word that contains the word family. Have children take turns filling in the blanks to complete the cheer. Make mini-megaphones out of rolled up paper. Shout it out!

⭐ 5 Using the Mini-Books

The mini-books are an excellent way to strengthen students' skills and encourage repeated readings to develop fluency. Here are some ideas for using the mini-books.

◆ After you've read a *Word Family Tales* book aloud several times, provide children with the mini-book. Children can then follow along in their mini-book as you read the story again. Model reading strategies along the way, such as how to sound out a word.

◆ Use the book as a basis for writing original stories. For example, have children extend the story's ending or use some of the word family words to create a new story.

⭐ 6 Assessment

The following suggestions will help you assess each child's reading skills, using the *Word Family Tales* books. Ask yourself:

◆ Does she recognize the word family in words?
◆ Can he read words with this spelling pattern?
◆ Can she spell words with this spelling pattern?
◆ What is the degree of automaticity, or speed, with which he can accomplish these tasks?

To Make the Mini-Books

1. Make double sided copies of the mini-book pages. (You should have two double-side copies for each one.)

2. Cut the pages in half along the dashed line.

3. Position the pages so that the lettered spreads (A, B, C, D) are face up. Place the B spread on top of the A spread. Then, place the C and D spread on top of those in sequence.

4. Fold the pages in half along the solid line. Make sure all the pages are in the proper order. Staple them together along the book's spine.

Quick-and-Easy Activities

"Three little letters, that's all we need, to make a whole family of words to read!" That's what your students will be cheering when they read each of the lively *Word Family Tales* stories. In this collection of 25 read-aloud stories, your students will meet Jumping Jill, Zelda Zink, Jan and her dog Stan, and other irresistible characters who will help them learn the 25 most frequently used word families. The easy-to-learn rhyming cheer at the end of each book will have students shouting "hooray" as they see how many new words they can read, write, and spell. Keep the momentum going with the skill-building activities that follow. You can use these whole class, small group, and independent activities with any of the stories to build on what students learn and have fun!

With the Class

What's the Word?

After sharing the story and letting children enjoy it, reread it, asking them to listen for words that are part of the featured word family. Let them give you a sign when they hear the words—for example, by waving their hands. Now, read the story a third time, this time stopping at words that belong to the word family and letting children chime in on them. If children need a clue, supply them with the initial sound—such as the j in Jill. With practice, children will be able to supply missing words more quickly and keep the story moving along. In the process, they'll develop an understanding of word parts and improve their literacy skills.

Buzzzz!

Play this lively game to reinforce words introduced in the *Word Family Tales* stories you share. Review the featured word-family chunk and the sound it makes—for example, -uck from *The Day Duck's Truck Got Stuck*. Explain to children that you are going to say some words that belong in this word family, but that you'll also say a word that doesn't belong. When they hear a word that doesn't belong, they need to "sound the buzzer" (by saying Buzzzz!) to let you know. For example, to reinforce the word family -uck, say duck, truck, stuck, muck, pluck, tock. When children hear *tock*, they say Buzzzz! Students will also enjoy taking a turn saying the words and inserting one that doesn't belong.

Pop-Up Words

This game reinforces recognition of familiar word parts.

Write words that contain the featured phonogram on index cards. Make one for each child. (If there are more children than words from a story, use the word list from the Reading Tips section in the back of the book as a source of additional words.) List the same words on a sheet of paper.

◆ Gather children in a seated circle and give each child a card. Explain that you're going to start a timer and say their words one at a time. When they hear their word, they hold up their card and pop up on their feet.

◆ Stop the timer when each child has popped up. How fast did the class recognize all of the words? Invite children to share strategies for improving their speed, then play again. Can they beat their time?

Line Up to Learn

While this transition activity gets children ready to move from one part of their day to the next, it will also help them recognize that word families are pronounced and spelled the same in every word in which they appear. After sharing a *Word Family Tales* story, write words that contain the featured phonogram on index cards. Punch holes at the top left and right corners and string with yarn to make necklaces. Give each child a necklace. When it's time to line up for lunch, recess, or other activities outside the classroom, have children put on their necklaces and listen while you call out the words one at a time. When children hear their word, have them spell it and get in line.

Est, Est, Pest!

Reinforce the phonograms students learn in the *Word Family Tales* stories with a fast-paced game they'll want to play again and again. It's a twist on the familiar and favorite "Duck, Duck, Goose." Your students will quickly catch on and be able to substitute new word families each time they play.

◆ After sharing a story, gather children in a seated circle. Review the featured word part, such as -est, and let children take turns thinking of words that have this sound and spelling pattern—for example, pest, nest, and best.

◆ Ask children if they remember how to play "Duck, Duck, Goose," then model the new version: Go around the circle, tapping children gently as you say est, est, est. When you tap a child and say a word with the -est sound—for example, best, that child gets up and chases you around the circle, trying to tag you before you sit in that child's space.

◆ If the child tags you first, that child sits back down and you repeat the procedure. If the child does not tag you, he or she goes around the circle, tapping children and repeating the -est sound, then saying a word in that word family—such as pest. The chase around the circle begins again, and the game continues.

In a Group

Spell and Yell

Lead students in the cheer that appears at the end of each story. Then let children work in small groups to create new cheers that reinforce the featured word family.

◆ After practicing the cheer that appears in the book, brainstorm other words that belong to the same word family. List them on the chalkboard.

◆ Divide the class into small groups and assign each group several of the new words. Have students write their new words on large index cards or tagboard and attach craft-stick handles to make signs.

◆ Have students in each group practice their cheer, then perform it for the class. When they come to line four of the cheer ("You'll find it in…"), have them hold up their signs one at a time, and, with class participation, spell and "yell" each new word.

Tip

Students can roll up construction paper in a cone shape and tape it in place to make megaphones to use with their cheers.

Silly Sentences

Students use rhyming words from a story to build silly sentences—and their ability to sound out and spell words.

◆ After sharing a story, let students revisit each page to find words with the featured spelling pattern. List the words on slips of paper.

◆ Divide the class into small groups and give each group a few slips of paper. Ask students in each group to come up with another three or four words that belong in the same word family.

◆ Have students use their words to build silly sentences, adding additional words, such as *the*, *of*, and *to*, as needed. For example, based on words from Jan and Stan, a group of students might write the following sentence: The snowman ran and began to fan the man in Japan.

◆ Let students write their sentences on sentence strips and share them with the class. Follow up by cutting apart the words in their sentences, then mixing them up and placing them in a center. Students can visit on their own and build more silly sentences, using words from all of the groups. Have chart paper handy so that students can record the sentences they create.

Word Family Mini-Plays

Bring stories to life by letting children work in small groups to create and perform mini-plays. Model the activity first by creating a mini-play and inviting a few students to help you act it out. Here's an easy one for three characters, based on the story *Jan and Stan.*

Jan: Hi, I'm Jan. This is my dog, Stan.

Stan: (He barks.)

Fran: Remember me, Stan? I'm Jan's friend Fran.

Stan: (He barks.)

Fran: Stan, do you and Jan want to play soccer?

Stan: (He barks enthusiastically.)

Jan: Stan, you look thirsty! Here's a soda. You can drink it from the can!

Fran: Jan, the phone's ringing.

Jan: That's my Grandma Nan. She likes to talk to Stan!

Stan: Hi, Grandma Nan. Guess what I did today. I played soccer with Jan and Fran, cooled off with a fan, cooked food in a pan, and took a ride in a van!

On Your Own

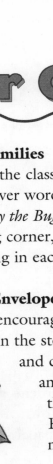

Lift-the-Flap Word Families

After sharing a story with the class, try this activity to encourage independent reading. Place small sticky notes over words in the story that contain the featured word family— for example, in *Billy the Bug's New Jug*, cover words that end in -ug. Place the book in a reading corner, and let children revisit it on their own, guessing the words that belong in each space and lifting the flaps to check their answers.

An Envelope of Words

To encourage children to practice the spelling patterns introduced in the stories, write words from a word family on sentence strips and cut apart each letter. Place the letters in an envelope and label it with the word family. Let children borrow the envelope and use the letters to build rhyming words. For additional practice, they can record the words they make on a sheet of paper.

Tip

To make an envelope of words for each child, write words (with each letter widely spaced) from the word family on a sheet of paper, then photocopy a class set. Give each child a copy of the words to cut apart and place in an envelope.

Word Family Collaborative Banner

After sharing a story, review the featured phonogram and invite children to list words from the story that have this sound. Let them suggest other words that have the same sound, too. Encourage children to spell the words as you write them on slips of paper. Place all of the words (make sure there's one for each child) in a bag and let children randomly choose one. Give each child a sheet of drawing paper. Have children write their word on the paper and draw a picture to illustrate it. When children are finished, have them arrange their papers side by side, then tape them together to make a banner. Display at children's eye level so that they can easily practice reading their words.

Getting More from the Word Family Tales Mini-Books

Children will delight in having their own copies of the stories. Try these suggestions to learn more with the mini-books.

This Book Belongs To...

Let children make bookplates to personalize their mini-books. On a label for each child, write "This book about the letters _____ belongs to _____." (Save time by creating labels on the computer and printing them by the sheet.) When you give students a new mini-book, have them complete a label and place it on the inside cover of their book. These fun bookplates will help prevent children from misplacing their books, and will reinforce spelling patterns, too.

See It, Spell It

Children will enjoy coloring in their mini-books from beginning to end. As they do so, have them look for things in the pictures on each page that represent the featured word family. For example, in *Jumping Jill Went Down the Hill*, children can find a picture of Jill and a hill on page 1. Jill appears again on page 2, a letter from Uncle Bill on page 3, and so on. For each thing in the picture they find, have them look for the matching word on the page, then circle and spell it aloud. How many picture and word matches can they make in the whole book?

Making Home-School Connections

The more practice children have with the spelling patterns in word families, the more familiar they'll become with using those chunks to read and write new words. Sending the mini-books home for students to share with families is one way to provide this practice. Use the badge (below) as a reminder for children to share the mini-books with their families. Photocopy a class set of the badges and trim to size. Let children color the badges, then write in the title of the mini-book (first space) and a sample word (second space) with the featured phonogram. Attach the badge to each child's shirt, jacket, or backpack when you send the mini-books home. Parents will come to recognize the badges and look forward to sharing the Word Family Tales mini-books their children bring home.

Look! Look! I have a new book!

It's called _____

_____ .

Let's read it and look for words that rhyme with _____!

-ai • -ay • -eep   -an • -ank • -at
-ice • -ide   -ap
-ice   -ack
-ine   -ock
-ake   -op
-est   -ot
-ell • -ing • -ink • -in • -uck • -ump • -ug • -ill

The Top 25 Word Families

-an

ban	pan	clan
can	ran	plan
Dan	tan	scan
fan	van	span
man	bran	than

-ank

bank	yank	Frank
Hank	blank	plank
lank	clank	prank
rank	crank	spank
sank	drank	thank
tank	flank	

-at

bat	pat	flat
cat	rat	scat
fat	sat	slat
gnat	vat	spat
hat	brat	that
mat	chat	

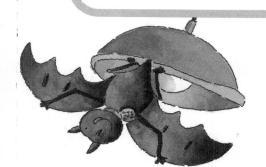

-ap

cap	sap	scrap
gap	tap	slap
map	yap	snap
lap	chap	strap
nap	clap	trap
rap	flap	wrap

-ack

back	quack	clack	smack
hack	rack	crack	snack
Jack	sack	knack	stack
lack	tack	shack	track
pack	black	slack	whack

-ock

dock	tock	smock
hock	block	stock
knock	crock	
lock	clock	
mock	flock	
rock	frock	
sock	shock	

-op

bop	top	prop
cop	chop	shop
hop	crop	slop
mop	drop	stop
pop	flop	
sop	plop	

-ot

cot	lot	clot
dot	not	plot
got	pot	shot
hot	rot	slot
jot	tot	spot
knot	blot	trot

-ill

ill	pill	skill
bill	quill	spill
dill	sill	still
fill	till	thrill
gill	will	trill
hill	chill	trill
Jill	drill	twill
kill	frill	
mill	grill	

-ing

bing	wing	sting
ding	zing	sring
king	bring	swing
ping	cling	thing
ring	fling	wring
sing	spring	

-ink

kink	rink	shrink
link	sink	slink
mink	wink	stink
pink	blink	think
	brink	
	clink	
	drink	

-in

bin	win	spin
fin	chin	thin
kin	grin	twin
pin	shin	
tin	skin	

-ip

dip	sip	drip	snip
hip	tip	flip	strip
lip	zip	grip	trip
nip	blip	ship	whip
quip	chip	skip	
rip	clip	slip	

-uck

buck	suck	stuck
duck	tuck	struck
luck	Chuck	truck
muck	cluck	
puck	pluck	

-ump

bump	lump	clump	slump
dump	pump	frump	stump
hump	rump	grump	thump
jump	chump	plump	trump

-ug

bug	pug	shrug
dug	rug	slug
hug	tug	smug
jug	chug	snug
lug	drug	thug
mug	plug	

-ell

bell	Nell	dwell
cell	sell	shell
dell	tell	smell
fell	well	spell
jell	yell	swell

-est

best	vest
jest	west
lest	zest
nest	chest
pest	crest
rest	quest
test	wrest

-ake

bake	lake	sake	drake	stake
cake	make	take	flake	
fake	quake	wake	shake	
Jake	rake	brake	snake	

-ine

dine	nine	shrine
fine	pine	spine
line	vine	swine
mine	shine	whine

-ice

dice	rice	splice
lice	vice	thrice
nice	price	twice
mice	slice	

-ide

hide	wide	slide
ride	bride	snide
side	glide	stride
tide	pride	

-ail

bail	nail	
fail	pail	wail
Gail	quail	flail
hail	rail	frail
jail	sail	snail
mail	tail	trail

-ay

bay	pay	play
day	ray	say
gay	say	spray
hay	way	stay
jay	clay	stray
lay	fray	sway
may	gray	tray
nay	play	

-eep

beep	keep	steep
bleep	peep	sweep
creep	seep	weep
deep	sheep	asleep
jeep	sleep	

The Mini-Books

-an

Give a great holler, a cheer, a yell

For all of the words that we can spell

With an A and an N that make the sound –an,

You'll find it in man and can and van.

Two little letters, that's all that we need

To make a whole family of words to read!

14

-an

Jan and Stan

by Samantha Berger
Illustrated by Rick Brown

And he definitely can't build a snowman.

Want to hear a secret about my dog Stan?
He thinks he can do everything that I can!

A

He loves to play soccer with my friend Fran.

B

He can't play checkers with my brother Dan.

He can't make music like I can.

Word Family Tales Teaching Guide Page 26

Want to hear another secret
about my dog Stan?
He can't really do everything that I can.

He drinks orange soda right out of the can.

He sits right up front
when we ride in the van.

He cools himself off with a little fan.

He lies in the sun to get a nice tan.

C

Woof! Woof!

He talks on the phone to Grandma Nan.

He likes his food heated up in a pan.

D

He reads comic books.
His favorite's Catman!

-ank

Give a great holler, a cheer, a yell

For all of the words that we can spell

With an A, N, and K that make the sound —ank,

You'll find it in bank and plank and clank.

Three little letters, that's all that we need

To make a whole family of words to read!

14

Hank's Bank

by Maxwell Higgins
Illustrated by R.W. Alley

CLINKITY-CLANK!

CLINKITY-CLANK CLINKITY-CLANK CLINKITY-CLANK

Now Frank doesn't mind
when Hank shakes his bank—
Frank's too busy making
his own CLINKITY-CLANK!

12

CLINKITY-CLANK!

This is Hank.
And this is Hank's bank.
Hank likes to shake and shake his bank
to hear the coins go clinkity-clank.

1

A

CLINKITY-CLANK! CLINKITY-CLANK!
CLINKITY-CLANK-CLANK-CLANK!
Nothing sounds better
than coins in a bank!

13

CLINKITY-CLANK! CLINKITY-CLANK!
Hank loves the sound of coins in his bank.

2

B

Yippee! Frank has his very own bank!
And for that, he has his brother to thank.

11

and comes home later
with a present for Frank.

CLINKITY-CLANK
CLINKITY-CLANK

This is Hank's big brother, Frank.
Frank covers his ears
when Hank shakes his bank.
He can't stand to hear
all that clinkity-clank.

"I'm awfully sorry," Frank tells Hank,
"But I was tired of all that clinkity-clank."

All afternoon, Hank looked for his bank.
When he couldn't find it, his heart just sank.

One day Frank decides to play a small prank.
He hides Hank's bank under a plank.

C

Then Hank gets an idea.
He runs off with his bank...

Frank feels bad when he sees Hank.
It wasn't very nice to hide his bank.

D

So Frank gives the plank a little yank,
and hands the bank right back to Hank.

-at

Give a great holler, a cheer, a yell

For all of the words that we can spell

With an A and a T that make the sound –at,

You'll find it in mat and cat and bat.

Two little letters, that's all that we need

To make a whole family of words to read!

14

-at

A Bat Named Pat

by Betsy Franco
Illustrated by Bari Weissman

I REALLY hate to be a brat,
but I want a bat,
and that is that!

12

My mother and I had a nice long chat
about getting a pet like a dog or a cat.

1

For my sister Hari,
who always wears a "hat"

A

Try as I might, Mom said no to the bat.
So I'd like you to meet
my new cat…named Pat!

13

But I told her, "I REALLY want a bat—
not a fish or a bird or a dog or a cat."

2

B

At first some kids
might want her to scat,
but after a while,
they'd start to love Pat.

11

On Show-and-Tell Day,
I'd wear a tall hat,
and on my shoulder,
there'd be Pat!

10

If I had a bat, I would name her Pat.
Her collar would say, "Pat the Bat."

3

...and swoop out the window,
just like that—
to meet her pals,
a nice bunch of bats.

8

I'd pet her little
head—pat, pat, pat.
I'd sing lullabies as
she sat on her mat.

5

I'd make her some supper—
two spiders, one gnat,
and all sorts of spooky bugs like that.

4

C

They'd flutter around like acrobats,
then sit in my tree for bat chitchats.

9

She'd sleep all day
with her wings folded flat—
I would always know
just where she was at!

6

D

But when the moon got round and fat,
she'd leave our bedroom habitat…

7

Give a great holler, a cheer, a yell

For all of the words that we can spell

With an A and a P that make the sound −ap,

You'll find it in cap and map and nap.

Two little letters, that's all that we need

To make a whole family of words to read!

A nap for Zap

by Kama Einhorn
Illustrated by Cynthia Jabar

"Then I'll…"
But something happened to little Zap.
He fell sound asleep in his Pap's lap.

There once was a firefly
whose name was Zap
and he never wanted to take his nap.

A

"Sleep tight, tiny chap,"
whispered Zap's happy Pap.

His father said, "Come sit on my lap.
Put out your light. Take your nap, little Zap!"

B

"Then I'll fly to London in my baseball cap—
I'll be sure to bring my map!"

"Then I'll eat a giant
gingersnap."

"Not now, Pap!" replied little Zap.
"I've got lots of plans! Flap, flap, flap."

"Then I'll balance
on a bottlecap."

"Then I'll build a boat.
Tap, tap, tap."

"First I'll visit the owl.
Yap, yap, yap."

C

"Then I'll cut paper dolls
from old gift wrap."

"Then I'll paint a house.
Slap, slap, slap."

D

"Then I'll make some music. Snap, snap, snap.
Then I'll put on a show. Clap, clap, clap."

Give a great holler, a cheer, a yell

For all of the words that we can spell

With an A, C, and K that make the sound –ack,

You'll find it in Mack and pack and snack.

Three little letters, that's all that we need

To make a whole family of words to read.

14

A Snack for Mack

by Cass Hollander
Illustrated by Rick Brown

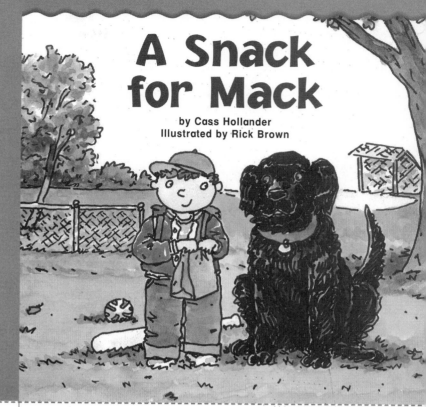

But when Jack dropped his
snack sack…

12

This is Jack and his black dog Mack.

1

A

Mack did NOT bring it back!

Jack has a knack for forgetting things.

B

Mack brought it back.

When Jack left his bike in the rack…

Mack has a knack for bringing them back.

When Jack left his backpack beside the track…

Mack brought it back.

When Jack hit the ball with a WHACK…

C

Mack brought it back.

When Jack left his books in a stack…

D

Mack brought them back.

Give a great holler, a cheer, a yell

For all of the words that we can spell

With an O, C, and K that make the sound —ock,

You'll find it in tock and block and clock.

Three little letters, that's all that we need

To make a whole family of words to read!

14

The Clock Who Could Not Tock

by Pamela Chanko
Illustrated by Liisa Chauncy Guida

The customer bought Tick and Tock. "I'll have the most unusual clocks on my block!" he said.

12

Once upon a time, there was an old clock shop. Inside the shop lived a whole flock of clocks. There were alarm clocks, cuckoo clocks, even a tall grandfather clock.

1

For Gatsby, with a heart like a rock,
may you never discover the meaning of "clock"

A

So Tick and Tock went home with the man.
There, the two friends ticked and tocked
around the clock and lived happily
ever after.

13

All day long, the shop was filled with the
sound of clocks. "Tick, tock. Tick, tock.
Tick, tock." But one clock stood out from
the rest. His name was Tick.

2

B

A customer heard the musical tick-tocking
of the two clocks working together.
"How lovely!" he said. "I've never seen
anything like that before." Tick was as
proud as a peacock. So was Tock.

11

Then the two clocks stood up tall, side by side. In perfect time came the sound of each clock, "Tick, tock. Tick, tock. Tick, tock."

10

Tick had a problem.
"Tick, tick. Tick, tick. Tick, tick."
Tick was a clock who could not tock!

3

The next morning, the clocks welcomed the new member of their flock. But they were in for quite a shock. When the clock opened her mouth, out came, "Tock, tock. Tock, tock. Tock, tock."

8

The other clocks began to tease Tick. "What good is a clock who can't tock?" they said. Tick hated being a laughing stock, but what could he do?

5

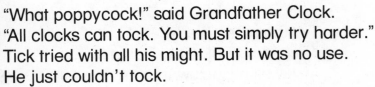

"What poppycock!" said Grandfather Clock.
"All clocks can tock. You must simply try harder."
Tick tried with all his might. But it was no use.
He just couldn't tock.

4

C

Tick couldn't believe it—a clock who could
only tock! This gave Tick an idea. He
whispered something to Tock, the new clock.

9

Then late one day, as the shopkeeper
was about to lock up, there was a
knock at the door. In walked a woman
carrying a pink clock.

6

D

The woman handed the clock to the
shopkeeper. "I don't like this clock," she said.
"Perhaps you can sell it to someone else."

7

Give a great holler, a cheer, a yell

For all of the words that we can spell

With an O and a P that make the sound –op,

You'll find it in hop and mop and stop.

Two little letters, that's all that we need

To make a whole family of words to read!

14

Bop, Bop at the Bunny Hop

by Robin C. Fitzsimmons
Illustrated by Ellen Joy Sasaki

Don't have a partner?
Just grab a mop!

12

Put down your work,
it's time to stop.
And tap your toes
at the Bunny Hop!

1

For Alex –
You're the TOP!

A

Everyone's hip at the Bunny Hop!

13

Hip! Hop! Hip! Hop!
Horses are hoofing at the Bunny Hop.
They do the purple-pony.
They just can't stop!

They'll dance all night,
until they drop.

2

B

11

Hop! Dop! Top! Flop!
Plop! Glop! Zop! Bop!

Dip! Dop! Dip! Dop!
Doggies are dancing at the Bunny Hop.
They do the beagle-boogie.
They just can't stop!

Zip! Zop! Zip! Zop!
Zebras are zooming at the Bunny Hop.
They do the ziggy-zag.
They just can't stop!

Flip! Flop! Flip! Flop!
Frogs are flying at the Bunny Hop.
They do the ribbit-rumba.
They just can't stop!

Tip! Top! Tip! Top!
Tigers are twisting at the Bunny Hop.
They do the jungle-jive.
They just can't stop!

4

Bip! Bop! Bip! Bop!
Bees are buzzing at the Bunny Hop.
They do the buggy-bumble.
They just can't stop!

9

Plip! Plop! Plip! Plop!
Penguins are prancing at the Bunny Hop.
They do the tuxedo-tango.
They just can't stop!

6

Glip! Glop! Glip! Glop!
Goldfish are grooving at the Bunny Hop.
They do the minnow-mambo.
They just can't stop!

7

Give a great holler, a cheer, a yell

For all of the words that we can spell

With an O and a T that make the sound –ot,

You'll find it in hot and pot and Scot.

Two little letters, that's all that we need

To make a whole family of words to read.

14

Scot and Dot

By Maxwell Higgins
Illustrated by Rusty Fletcher

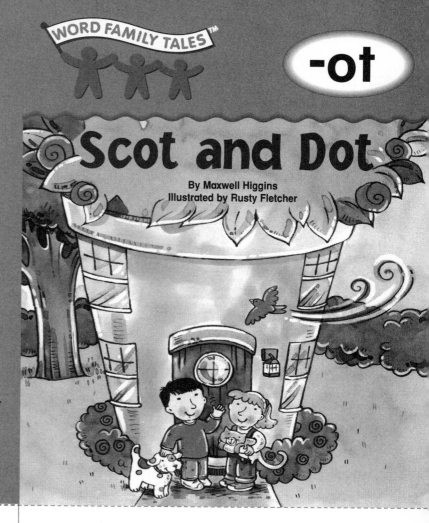

The kids who once teased them,
now do not.

12

There once was a tot
whose name was Scot.
He had a dog whose name was Spot.

1

A

They wish they had homes like Scot
and Dot!

13

They lived together in a flowerpot,
the tot named Scot and his good dog Spot.

2

B

On chilly days, Scot visits Dot
for tea and cake in the big teapot.

11

Now, when the weather is sunny and hot,
Dot visits Scot in his flowerpot.
They plant petunias and forget-me-nots.
(Apricot and Spot help out a lot!)

The girl who lived next door to Scot
teased him for living in a flowerpot.
But this didn't bother Scot one jot—
he liked his home an awful lot.

Then Scot told Dot, right on the spot,
all about his home in the flowerpot.

They lived together in a big teapot,
the tot named Dot and sweet Apricot.

There once was a tot
whose name was Dot.
She had a cat named Apricot.

"I love your house!" Dot told Scot.
(As a matter of fact, so did Apricot!)

The boy who lived next door to Dot
teased her for living in a big teapot.
But this didn't bother Dot one jot—
she liked her home an awful lot.

One day when Scot was walking Spot,
he passed right by the big teapot.
"I love your house!" Scot told Dot.
(As a matter of fact, so did Spot!)

-ill

Give a great holler, a cheer, a yell

For all of the words that we can spell

With an I, L, and L that make the sound —ill,

You'll find it in Jill and hill and thrill.

Three little letters, that's all that we need

To make a whole family of words to read!

14

-ill

Jumping Jill
Went Down the Hill

by Maria Fleming
Illustrated by Bari Weissman

And if you haven't seen her lately…

12

Once upon a time
there was a girl named Jill.
She lived inside a little house
that sat upon a hill.

1

A

you can bet she's jumping still!

One spring day, a package came.
It was addressed to Jill.

B

Jill jumped down the front porch steps,
then jumped right down the hill.

She hopped back on her pogo stick
and went jumping out the door.

What could it be? A pogo stick
from dear ol' Uncle Bill!

Her mother called the doctor,
who came over right away.
He handed Jill a pill and said,
"You'll feel better in a day."

Jill jumped and jumped and jumped all day.
Her mother begged, "Sit still!"
But there was just no stopping
that jolly jumper, Jill.

Jill hopped right on that pogo stick.
It didn't take much skill.
She found that jumping up and down
gave her quite a thrill.

That little pill, it did the trick.
Jill felt better than before!

Even as she ate her lunch,
up and down she hopped.
Jill jumped as she drank her milk,
and didn't spill a drop!

But then Jill got a funny look.
"I feel ill," she said.
Jill hopped right off her pogo stick
and climbed right into bed.

Give a great holler, a cheer, a yell

For all of the words that we can spell

With an I, N, and G that make the sound –ing,

You'll find it in king and ring and sing.

Three little letters, that's all that we need

To make a whole family of words to read!

14

-ing

Spring in the Kingdom of Ying

by Liza Charlesworth
Illustrated by Ellen Joy Sasaki

For all of the land is loaded with zing—

Yippee! It's spring in the Kingdom of Ying!

To Ingrid Kemperman—
A friendship with zing
is a wonderful thing!

A

what a wonderful, wonderful, wonderful thing!

The striped bells of the tower begin to ring.

B

bringing a smile to the face of the king.

beckoning the blue jay to wave "Hi" with her wing,

The polka-dot bullfrogs all start to sing.

The rooster unwinds his great ball of string,

The teeny-weeny raindrops whisper,
"ping, ping, ping."

The courteous cows push pigs on a swing.

C

sending his kite up in the air on a fling,

The very happy honeybees decide not to sting.

D

Two dogs make bouquets
from the daisies cats bring.

Give a great holler, a cheer, a yell

For all of the words that we can spell

With an I, N, and K that make the sound –ink,

You'll find it in pink and mink and think.

Three little letters, that's all that we need

To make a whole family of words to read!

14

When Zelda Zink Spilled Purple Ink

by Liza Charlesworth
Illustrated by Matt Phillips

"Why, that is soooooo precious!"
squealed Mimi Mink.
The tears of joy made her blink.

12

The instant she got back from vacation,
Zelda Zink phoned her best friend Mimi Mink…

1

To my perfect pal,
Sarah Rae Trousdale

A

Then Mimi put the T-shirt
on Fifi La Frink
who barked a BIG thank
you to dear Zelda Zink—
who was now rather happy
she spilled purple ink!

13

and said, "Can you drop by this afternoon?
You can bring your toy poodle, Fifi La Frink."

2

B

What to do? What to do?
Zelda had to think.
"I brought it back from vacation…
isn't it perfect for… Fifi La Frink?"

11

They hugged hello, then
Mimi asked:
"What's that teeny T-shirt
from the Island of Tink?"

You see, Zelda had a great gift for her pal:
a souvenir T-shirt from the Island of Tink.

Quick as a wink,
she tossed it in the washer and dryer.
And the pink disappeared,
but did that shirt ever shrink!

Quick as a wink,
she scrubbed the shirt
with some toothpaste
she found by the sink.

But before her guests arrived,
Zelda spilled a bottle—
covering the shirt with purple ink!

C

"Clink! Clink!" went the doorbell.
Oh no—it's Mimi Mink!

And the ink disappeared,
but now the shirt
had a peppermint stink!

D

Quick as a wink,
she doused it with cherry drink.
And the smell disappeared,
but the shirt turned bright pink!

-in

Give a great holler, a cheer, a yell

For all of the words that we can spell

With an I and an N that make the sound –in,

You'll find it in win and pin and twin.

Two little letters, that's all that we need

To make a whole family of words to read.

14

-in

Lin and Min Are Twins

by Pamela Chanko
Illustrated by Cary Pillo

Yes, each of us is an identical twin.
We're the same outside,
but a bit different in.

My name is Lindy, but they call me Lin.
My name is Mindy, but they call me Min.

For Catherine, my twin within

A

And here's one more fact
that really makes us grin—
We both love each other
through thick and through thin!

13

Each of us is an identical twin.
We have the same nose
and we have the same chin.

2

B

And Lin collects shells in a little tin.
She's a basketball star—she gets it right in!

11

Min plays music on the violin
and sometimes she wears a dinosaur pin.

And when we feel silly,
we have the same grin.

We both have a goldfish
with one purple fin.
They're named after us:
Little Lin, Little Min.

We love to go bowling.
We both play to win.
And can you believe it—
we knock down the same pin!

We're both kind of tall
and a little bit thin.
We each have eleven freckles
on our skin!

But there are ways you can tell
which twin is which twin.
Do you really want to know?
Okay, let's begin.

Our town has a parade that we're always in.
We both twirl batons—
we really make them spin!

-ip

Give a great holler, a cheer, a yell

For all of the words that we can spell

With an I and a P that make the sound –ip,

You'll find it in sip and hip and trip.

Two little letters, that's all that we need

To make a whole family of words to read!

14

-ip

Take a Trip to Planet Blip

by Kama Einhorn
Illustrated by Matt Phillips

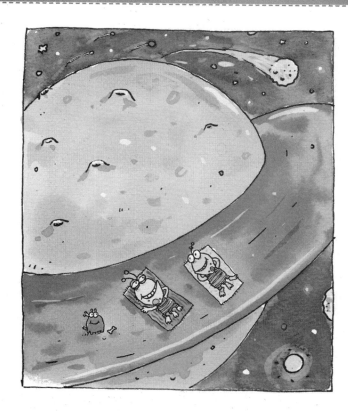

then watch the comets whirl and whip.

Hi, Earthlings, my name is Zip.
Come visit me on Planet Blip.

A

Oh, please do visit Planet Blip.
You'll love it here. You'll really flip!

13

We'll zoom around in my spaceship.

2

B

We'll jump in the middle to take a dip...

11

We'll hike 'round a crater—
be careful, don't slip!

You'll see cool sights on our little trip!

Instead of barking, he says, "Mip! Mip!"
Instead of running, he likes to skip.

and have a moonball championship.

We'll drop by to visit my buddy Kip…

C

When we curl his hair, he looks really hip.

The loser buys ice cream—quadruple dip!
(Just be careful not to drip!)

D

You'll meet my pet. He's called a pip.

Give a great holler, a cheer, a yell

For all of the words that we can spell

With a U, C, and K that make the sound –uck,

You'll find it in duck and luck and truck.

Three little letters, that's all that we need

To make a whole family of words to read!

14

The Day Duck's Truck Got Stuck

by Maria Fleming
Illustrated by Rusty Fletcher

Duck thanked all the animals for helping her free her truck from the muck. Then she gave ice-cream cones to everyone.

12

This is Duck. She drives an ice-cream truck.

1

A

And little Chickadee
got the tallest cone of all.

One day, Duck was driving her truck in the rain. She drove right into a big mud puddle. Now Duck's truck was stuck in the muck!

The sun's bright rays dried up all the mud and muck. Finally, Duck's truck came unstuck! "Hooray for Chickadee!" the animals cheered. "What good luck that you came along!"

B

But Chickadee was sure he could help.
In a tiny voice, he began to sing,
"Chick-a-dee-dee-dee."
Chickadee's song was so cheerful that the
sun came out from behind a cloud to hear it.

✶10

"Yuck!" said Duck, stepping into the muck.
"What bad luck!" Duck tried to push her truck
out of the muck. But the truck stayed stuck.

3✶

Suddenly, a small voice said, "I can help
you get the truck out of the muck."
It was little Chickadee. The other animals
looked at Chickadee and laughed.

✶8

Duck and Porcupine pushed and pushed.
But the truck stayed stuck. Just then,
Woodchuck came riding along on her scooter.
"Looks like you could use some help," said
Woodchuck.

5✶

Duck saw Porcupine walking along
the side of the road.
"Porcupine, will you help me push my truck
out of the muck?" asked Duck.
"I'd be happy to," said Porcupine.

C

"Chickadee, you're so small," said Duck.
"How could you help move this big
truck?"

9

Duck, Porcupine, and Woodchuck
pushed as hard as they could. But that
truck stayed stuck.

D

6

Before long, Moose came strolling by.
He offered to help, too. Then Duck,
Porcupine, Woodchuck, and Moose
pushed with all their might. But the
truck stayed stuck.

7

-ump

Give a great holler, a cheer, a yell

For all of the words that we can spell

With a U, M, and P that make the sound –ump,

You'll find it in bump and lump and jump.

Three little letters, that's all that we need

To make a whole family of words to read!

14

-ump

The Day Mr. Gump Helped Katie Krump

by Gale Clifford
Illustrated by Paige Billin-Frye

"Why, you've made a fine table!"
cried a thrilled Katie Krump.

12

Is something broken? Then call Mr. Gump!
He can fix everything and is never a grump!

1

To Guy, my favorite Mr. Gump

A

"And it's just time for tea now,
my dear Mr. Gump!
Tell me, how do you take yours—
with one or two lumps?"

He can fix a flat tire.
He uses his pump!

B

And when he was finished,
he unveiled the stump...

He spackled and sanded
and smoothed every bump!

He can fix a thin pillow.
He makes it quite plump!

So he zoomed right over
to Miss Katie Krump's,
who showed him the stump,
which was loaded with lumps.

He can even fix a pogo stick.
He puts back the jump!

He can fix a stuffed camel.
He sews up its hump!

C

But he knew he could fix it,
that great Mr. Gump.
So he took out his hammer.
Thump! Thump! Thump!

One day, Katie Krump called her pal Mr. Gump:
"Can you please take a look at my ugly tree
stump. If you can't repair it—it's going
to the dump!"

D

"I'm sure I can fix it," declared Mr. Gump
(for he hated to see anything go to the dump).

Give a great holler, a cheer, a yell

For all of the words that we can spell

With a U and a G that make the sound –ug,

You'll find it in bug and jug and rug.

Two little letters, that's all that we need

To make a whole family of words to read!

14

Billy the Bug's New Jug

by Wendy Cheyette Lewison

Illustrated by Maxie Chambliss

where they glugged grape soda
from Billy's new jug,
and sipped hot cocoa
from a bright yellow mug.

12

Billy the Bug lived in a rug.
Billy the Bug was a very snug bug.

1

To my husband, with a big bug hug

A

And they did the hokey-pokey and the jitterbug
and gave the little blue bug
a HUMONGOUS hug!

13

Under his rug were things that he'd dug.
He had all that he needed, except for a jug.

2

B

So the three gave the jug
a BIG, BIG, BIG tug
and were able to lug it
right back to the rug…

11

"Would you like to come over and visit my rug?"
kind Billy asked of the little blue bug.
"Oh yes," he replied, "It sounds very snug!"

He looked and looked
'til he found a fine jug.
Now he just had to lug it
back to his rug.

And out of the jug
popped a blue water bug!

Then Sally the Slug crawled out of her mug
and asked, "Can I help you lug that jug?"
"Well, that would be splendid!"
said Billy the Bug.

So Billy the Bug
gave the jug a BIG tug.
But the jug was too heavy
for one bug to lug.

 4

C

"Boy, it was lonely inside of that jug
with no one to hug!" said the little
blue bug.

9

So Sally the Slug and Billy the Bug
both gave that jug a BIG, BIG tug.
But the jug was too heavy
for the two pals to lug.

6

D

Then Sally the Slug saw a plug in the jug
and decided to give it a tremendous tug.
Water came gushing —
GLUG, GLUG, GLUG!

7

Give a great holler, a cheer, a yell

For all of the words that we can spell

With an E, L, and L that make the sound –ell,

You'll find it in bell and well and shell.

Three little letters, that's all that we need

To make a whole family of words to read!

14

Please Don't Tell About Mom's Bell

by Samantha Berger
Illustrated by Rick Brown

"Look what I have—my silver bell!
I got it fixed because it fell.
It's as good as new. You can't even tell!"

I have a secret, please don't tell!
I cannot find Mom's silver bell!

For the sweet Kama E.,
who's doing so well it makes me kvell

A

All this time she had the bell!
Wow, this story turned out swell!

13

I looked EVERYWHERE for that pretty bell.
I looked very, very, VERY well.

B

"Hi there, honey.
How's my Nell?"

 2

11

Oh no! That's Mom now! I can tell!

But I cannot find Mom's silver bell.

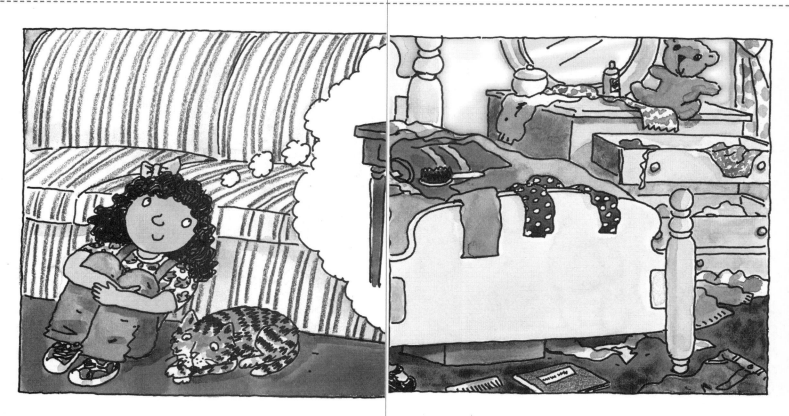

Mom really, really, loves that bell.
She always says, "Be careful, Nell."

But I cannot find Mom's silver bell.

I looked on the floor in case it fell.
I looked inside my turtle's shell!

Oh where, oh where, is that silver bell?

I even looked where my cat likes to dwell...

but I just can't find Mom's silver bell.
Please, oh please, pretty please, don't tell!

Give a great holler, a cheer, a yell

For all of the words that we can spell

With an E, S, and T that make the sound –est,

You'll find it in nest and vest and best.

Three little letters, that's all that we need

To make a whole family of words to read!

14

The Pest in the Nest

by Lisa Eve Huberman
Illustrated by Matt Phillips

Next Susie said,
"Stella, you aren't a pest.
You're a very fun friend—
I think YOU'RE the best!"

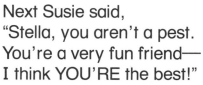12

Susie lived alone
in a neat little nest.
She was a very fine bird
with a bright pink crest.

1

To Ella and Sophie, the best in my nest

A

When the visit was over,
before Stella flew West,
she hugged her pal Susie.
She then hugged the nest!

13

One fine day,
Susie invited a guest—
and her bird-friend Stella
flew in from the West.

2

B

Stella the bird hid her beak in her vest.
"I'm so very sorry I was such a pest.
I just got so excited
'cause you are the best!"

11

"Stella," cried Susie,
"I have to protest!
You've brought nothing but trouble
into my nest!"

Stella wore sneakers
and a polka-dot vest.
She had curly green feathers
and a pretty blue crest.

When Susie showed Stella
her costume chest,
Stella scattered clothing
north, east, south and west!

When Susie served salad
and worms to her guest,
Stella gobbled her snack
and then finished the rest!

Susie thought Stella
was simply the best.
She didn't know Stella
would be such a pest.

When Susie lay down
to take a short rest
Stella woke her right up
by braiding her crest!

When Susie and Stella
had a painting contest,
Stella splattered purple
all over the nest!

When Susie had to study
for an arithmetic test,
Stella decided
to tap dance with zest!

-ake

Give a great holler, a cheer, a yell

For all of the words that we can spell

With an A, K, and E that make the sound –ake,

You'll find it in cake and rake and Jake.

Three little letters, that's all that we need

To make a whole family of words to read!

14

-ake

Jake's Cake Mistake

by Betsy Franco
Illustrated by Paul Harvey

But his friends all cheered,
"This is no mistake…

12

Jake the Snake
lived at the lake.
One day he decided
to bake a cake.

1

For my Bubby, Jessie
who baked great cakes

A

We'll just stand on our heads,
and eat RIGHT-SIDE-UP cake!"

13

But what kind of cake
did Jake want to make?
It had to be special
for his friends at the lake.

2

B

Now the super surprise
from Jake the Snake
was a big-gloppy-gooey
UPSIDE-DOWN-CAKE!

11

But he'd run out of time,
so he had to take
that very same cake
to his friends at the lake.

First he gathered up leaves
with a little rake,
then mushed in real mud—
it couldn't be fake!

And he topped it all off
with frilly snowflakes.
But then Jake the Snake
made a big mistake…

"I'll add yummy beetles
for the duck and the drake,
and some wiggly worms
for my bird friend, Blake."

"Froggie loves flies,"
thought Jake the Snake.
"And mouse will want berries
inside his cake!"

He dropped the cake—
for goodness' sake!

"The fish will want water
straight from the lake.
And I'll add gobs of honey
for bumblebee's sake!"

He shook the whole mixture.
Shake, shake, shake!

Give a great holler, a cheer, a yell

For all of the words that we can spell

With an I, N, and E that make the sound –ine,

You'll find it in fine and mine and dine.

Three little letters, that's all that we need

To make a whole family of words to read!

14

Dine With Nine Messy Monsters

by Liza Charlesworth
Illustrated by Matt Phillips

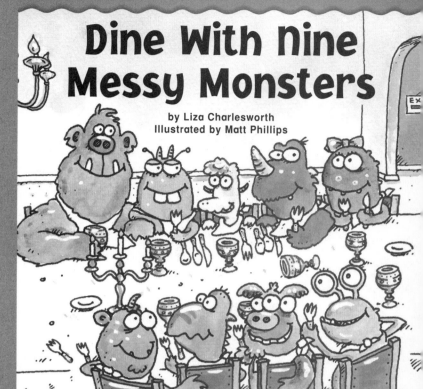

The smell was stupendous,
it was so divine…

12

In the mood for a meal that was
simply divine,
nine messy monsters sat
waiting to dine.

1

To Justin – My very favorite
messy monster!

A

Instead of one monster,
there were suddenly nine!

13

But one got scared off by a sharp porcupine!

2

B

There were bat lips and turnips
and frog legs so fine,
cold spider ice cream and warm
goblin spine!

11

One messy monster was waiting to dine,
"Yippee!" he said, "The meal is all mine!"

Eight messy monsters were waiting to dine,
but one swung away on a slippery vine!

Three messy monsters were waiting to dine,
but one got sleepy and went home to recline!

Six messy monsters were waiting to dine,
but one went to play with his pal, Frank N. Stine!

Seven messy monsters were waiting to dine,
but one felt his shoes really needed a shine!

C

Two messy monsters were waiting to dine,
But "The Mummy" was showing, so one got in line!

Five messy monsters were waiting to dine,
but one rolled away in a big ball of twine!

D

Four messy monsters were waiting to dine,
but one left to read his mushy valentine!

Give a great holler, a cheer, a yell

For all of the words that we can spell

With an I, C, and E that make the sound –ice,

You'll find it in mice and nice and twice.

Three little letters, that's all that we need

To make a whole family of words to read!

14

Chicken Soup With Rice and Mice

by Maria Fleming
Illustrated by Ellen Joy Sasaki

"That wasn't very nice," the mice scolded the cat. Then they pushed the cat out the door and slammed it behind her.
"She'll think twice before she comes in here again," they said.

12

Once there were two mice who had a restaurant.
One day, a cat walked in.
"I'll have chicken soup with rice," the cat said.

1

A

And that was the last the mice ever saw
of the cat. Although, they still get their
share of picky customers.

13

The mice brought the cat a big bowl of soup.
But when the cat tasted it, she made a face.
"If you want my advice, it needs more spice,"
said the cat.

"YEEEEEE-OWWWWWW!" the cat yelled
as she slipped on the ice.

2

B

11

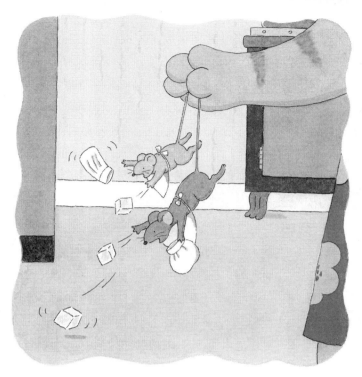

Suddenly, the mice remembered
the ice cubes under their hats.
Quick as a flash, they tossed them on the floor.

⭐10

So the mice went back to the kitchen.
They added a pinch more spice to the soup.
"Mmmmmmm, very nice," they agreed.

3⭐

The cat grabbed the soup bowl.
Then she grabbed the mice.
"Yum! Chicken soup with mice," said the
cat. "Now that's a dish I know I'll like!"

⭐8

The mice went back to the kitchen to
slice some onions and dice some carrots.
They threw them in the soup pot and took a taste.
"Very nice!" they agreed.

5⭐

"Try it now," the mice said to the cat.
She ate a spoonful.
"There's still something missing," the cat said.
"Maybe it needs some vegetables."

4

C

The cat started walking back to the table.
The mice knew they had better think fast.

9

But that cat was one picky customer.
She still didn't like the soup!
By now, the mice were tired and hot.
They put ice on their heads to cool off.
They sat down to think.

6

D

Just then, the cat peeked into the kitchen.
She looked at the bowl of soup on the counter.
She looked at the mice.
"I think I know what the soup needs," said the cat.

7

-ide

Give a great holler, a cheer, a yell

For all of the words that we can spell

With an I, D, and E that make the sound —ide,

You'll find it in ride and hide and slide.

Three little letters, that's all that we need

To make a whole family of words to read!

14

-ide

Ride and Slide

by Samantha Berger
Illustrated by R.W. Alley

Play 'til it's time to go back inside.

12

What can you do
when the snow falls outside,
and covers everything
far and wide?

1

For my dog Zeke, who loves to slide, ride, and hide in the snow outside

A

Fall fast asleep with your dog by your side.

 13

Put on your snow boots and step outside

 2

B

Make some snow angels
with wings deep and wide.

11

Play on the ice. Run, slip, and slide!

as your dog follows you, stride for stride.

Make a snow couple,
who stand side by side.

Build a cool snow fort
where your dog can hide.

Make a huge snowball
and toss it with pride.

Have a snow wedding
for the snow groom and bride.

4

C

9

Climb on a sled and go for a ride!

Put on some skis and take a long glide.

6

D

7

Give a great holler, a cheer, a yell

For all of the words that we can spell

With an A, I, and L that make the sound —ail,

You'll find it in pail and snail and tail.

Three little letters, that's all that we need

To make a whole family of words to read!

14

Snail Mail

by Maria Fleming
Illustrated by Rusty Fletcher

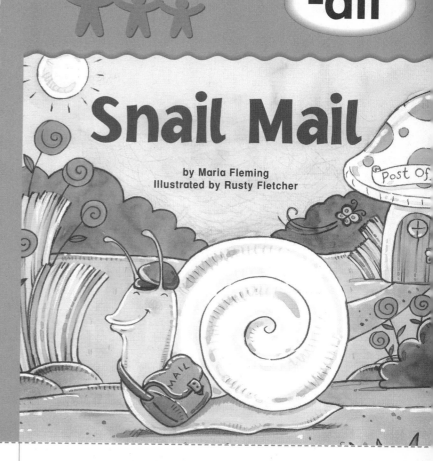

Then Snail borrows a hammer and a nail from Frog. He nails the sail in place.

12

Snail loves his job delivering the mail.
Through rain, sleet, snow, and hail,
Snail delivers the mail without fail!

1

A

Snail climbs aboard his new boat. Now he can sail down the trail with the mail!
"I'll never be late with the mail again!" Snail says happily. And he isn't—not even when it hails!

13

Snail follows a trail through the forest as he brings letters to all the animals.

2

B

Next, Snail finds a fat twig. "Now I just need to attach the sail to this twig!"

11

Snail pulls a leaf from a plant.
"This will make a perfect sail for a boat!"

There's just one problem. Snail is slow.
Very . . . very . . . very slow. And the mail
is always late. Very late.

Snail hates being late. He starts to wail.
"I am the worst mail snail that ever lived!"
he cries. Snail cries so hard, his tears
make a little stream.

"I didn't know today was your birthday!"
Snail says cheerfully.
"It isn't," Quail huffs. "My birthday was
three months ago! Snail, you are late
with the mail again!"

One day, Snail delivers a birthday card to Quail...

C

The stream of tears gives Snail an idea! Snail finds an old pail. He adds pail after pail of water from the pond to make his stream. Soon the stream becomes a river.

Snail feels terrible about the late card. He slides sadly along the trail. Finally, he reaches Frog's pond.

D

"I have a postcard from your aunt," Snail says. "When is she getting back from vacation?" "She's been back for five months!" Frog croaks. "Snail, you are late with the mail again!"

-ay

Give a great holler, a cheer, a yell

For all of the words that we can spell

With an A and a Y that make the sound —ay,

You'll find it in hay and way and May.

Two little letters, that's all that we need

To make a whole family of words to read!

-ay

Spend a Day in Backwards Bay

by Samantha Berger
Illustrated by Rick Brown

In the evening, folks have breakfast,
and after that they say—

In a distant land, far, far away,
is a little town called Backwards Bay.

A

"Rise and shine! Good morning!
See you yesterday!"

The folks who live in Backwards Bay
say "Goodnight" to start the day!

B

And every day but ONE is your birthday!

During class, the teacher asks,
"Who's teaching today?"

They put on their clothing the opposite way.

School doesn't begin until after kids play!

People heat up their water in an ice-cube tray!

A big turkey dinner's the first meal of the day!

C

The school bus backs up,
and they're on their way!

They comment, "Nice weather!"
when it's raining and gray.

D

They hold their umbrellas
to catch all the spray!

-eep

Give a great holler, a cheer, a yell

For all of the words that we can spell

With an E, E, and P that make the sound –eep,

You'll find it in jeep and sheep and sleep.

Three little letters, that's all that we need

To make a whole family of words to read!

14

-eep

To Sleep, Count Sheep

by Maria Fleming
Illustrated by Cary Pillo

Ten sheep fast asleep...

12

When the night is long and you can't sleep,
just lie in bed and count some sheep.

1

A

just like this boy—
shhh! Don't make a peep!

13

One sheep in a jeep.

2

B

Cheep!

CHEEP! CHEEP! CHEEP!

11

Nine sheep feeding chickens—

Two sheep in a traffic jam—
BEEP! BEEP! BEEP!

Seven sheep on a hill that's steep.

Four sheep dust and sweep.

Three sheep sit and weep.

Eight sheep quietly creep.

Five sheep visit Little Bo Peep.

Six sheep in the ocean deep.

Certificate of Completion

✗✗✗

This certificate is awarded to

_____

for successful completion of the Word Family Tales program.

You did it!

notes